My Natural and
The Spiritual EXPERIENCE

RAY ROBINSON

Order this book online at www.trafford.com
or email orders@trafford.com

Most Trafford titles are also available at major online book retailers.

Printed in the United States of America.

ISBN: 978-1-4907-1682-4 (sc)
ISBN: 978-1-4907-1681-7 (e)

Trafford rev. 03/11/2014

www.trafford.com

North America & international
toll-free: 1 888 232 4444 (USA & Canada)
fax: 812 355 4082

THIS BOOK IS IN RELATIONS TO ANYONE WHO'S GOING

THROUGH DIFFICULT SEASONS IN THEIR LIVES.

JUST BELIEVE IN THE WORD OF GOD FOR WHAT'S TAKING

PLACE IN ALL AREAS OF YOUR LIVES.

THIS IS ALSO TO ENCOURAGE YOUR SPIRIT THAT YOU ARE NOT ALONE

WITH THE MANY BURDENS OF LIFE.

IN ALL THAT HAPPENS,

I WILL TRUST GOD

I'VE GOT TO TRUST GOD

I MUST TRUST GOD

I AM GOING TO TRUST IN GOD

IN WHAT EVER HE SAYS CONCERNING ME.

THIS IS ABOUT MY BATTLE TO LIVE AND NOT DIE, IN MY

DOUBT

PROBLEMS

WORRIES

REJECTIONS

CONSPIRACY

BACK STABBERS

LIES

HATERS

SINS

AND MY HAVING NOTHING,

BUT LIVE BY THE WORD OF GOD.

KNOWING THAT EVERYTHING'S WORKING,

[THE GOOD, THE BAD, AND THE UGLY]

TOGETHER FOR MY GOOD.

I PRAY THAT THIS BOOK BLESSES

YOU IN YOUR LIFE'S JOURNEY.

HELPING YOU TO FIND THE ONE TRUE GOD

WHO HAS PATIENCE AND IS WAITING FOR YOU.

BLESS HIS HOLY NAME.

I PRAY THAT THESE TESTIMONIES WILL INSPIRE

AND ENCOURAGE ALL WHO READS IT.

THAT THE GRACE OF GOD IS

"SUFFICIENT" JUST FOR YOU".

I ALSO PRAY THAT NOTHING, BUT NOTHING, SHALL

SEPARATE ALL OF US FROM THE TRUE LOVE OF GOD.

AMEN . . .

Ray Robinson   12:51 PM 7/10/2012

ACKNOWLEDGEMENTS

I THANK GOD

THE CREATOR OF ALL THINGS

THE FATHER OF US ALL

MY LORD AND SAVIOR

JESUS THE CHRIST

THE ANOINTED ONE

AND HIS ANOINTING

AND THE HOLY SPIRIT

THE COMFORTER

MY LOVELY WIFE LINDA

OUR CHILDREN-GRAND CHILDREN

BISHOP ROBERT GATHERS JR.

MINISTER GWENDOLYN GATHERS

PASTOR ANTONIO GATHERS—FAMILY

MS. CYNTHIA M. ROBINSON

MR. ALVIN ROBINSON—FAMILY

MR. HENRY ROBINSON—FAMILY

MR. SAMUEL ROBINSON—FAMILY

MOTHER PEARL HILL—FAMILY

BROTHER RONNIE-COUSIN LYNN

[SPIRITUAL BROTHERS IN CHRIST JESUS]

MR. WENDELL WARREN

MR. WAYNE DAVID

[SPECIAL FAMILY]

MR. LEROY BATTS—MRS. LILLIAN BATTS

[SPIRITUAL HUSBAND-N-WIFE IN CHRIST JESUS]

MR. VIRGIL SMALLS—MRS. CAROLYN SMALLS

MR. CYRUS CHAMPANGE—MRS. EAVERNE CHAMPANGE

MR. STEVEN ARCHIE—MRS. KIM ARCHIE

MR. PAUL BROWN—MRS. PHYLECIA BROWN

I HAVE THE PLEASURE OF EXPERIENCING REAL GODLY LOVE BY THEM ALL

THEY ARE ALL NEAR AND DEAR TO MY HEART.

I THANK GOD FOR

THE CONGREGATION

THE ELDERS

BISHOP BRAIN D. MOORE

FIRST LADY JEMETTA MOORE,

THE MUSICIANS

THE TEACHINGS

THE USHERS

THE DEACONS

THE CHILDREN MINISTRY

THE BIBLE STUDIES

THE PRAISE-N-WORSHIP MINISTRY,

THE LIFE CENTER CATHEDRALS CHURCH MOTHERS

AND THE MINISTERS.

WITHOUT THE EXPERIENCES OF ALL THEIR SUPPORT IN ALL

MY AFFLICTIONS

DENIAL

STRUGGLES

SHORT COMINGS

TESTS

REJECTIONS

TRIALS AND TRIBULATIONS

ALL THE DEVIL HAS TRIED TO BEAT ME DOWN WITH,

TO MAKE ME GIVE UP WHAT GOD HAVE JUST FOR ME.

THIS WOULD NOT BE.

THIS MINISTRY THAT I AM UNDER, HAS BEEN A WONDERFUL

EXPERIENCE FOR ME, HELPING ME TO GET IN POSITION

TO BE USED BY CHRIST JESUS.

THEY HAVE TRULY BLESSED ME TO CHASE AFTER CHRIST.

I LOVE, LOVE, LOVE THEM ALL FOR BEING THERE FOR ME.

THIS IS A LOVE THAT I HAVE NEVER FELT BEFORE IN ALL MY

DAYS.

TO ALL THAT READS MY LIFE'S TESTIMONIES

OF HOW I CAME TO CHRIST AND GOT BETTER IN THE SPIRIT

THAN I USE TO BE IN THE NATURAL,

REMEMBER THIS;

THE DEVIL IS A LIAR!

I PRAY THAT THE FATHER OF US ALL WILL KEEP US IN UNITY,

AT LIFE CENTER CATHEDRAL AS

ONE WITH EACH OTHER

ONE IN CHRIST

ONE IN GOD.

I WOULD LIKE FOR YOU TO USE YOUR IMAGINATION AS YOU

READ EACH STORY. PLACE YOUR SELF IN THESE SITUATIONS

AND THE MESSAGE WILL BE REVEALED TO YOU.

I PRAY THAT THIS BOOK WILL BE PRINTED AND PUBLISHED

IN EVERY KNOWN LANGUAGES ACROSS THIS WORLD.

AMEN.

RAY ANTHONY ROBINSON   9/ 3 / 2013   11:39 AM

INTRO TO BOOK

[EL-ROI] THE GOD THAT SEES, THE OMNISCIENCE]

THIS BOOK IS ABOUT MY EXPERIENCE-EXPRESSIONS IN LIFE;

IN THE NATURAL AND IN THE SPIRITUAL FORM;

MY TESTIMONIES.

IT'S ABOUT

MY HEALTH FAILING

BECAUSE OF POSTURAL STRAIN,

MYOSITIS, SEGMENTAL/SOMATIC

DYSFUNC, LUMBAR (MCP), NEURITIS

RADICULITIS, UNSPEC. LUMAR

THOR (MC2) SCOLIOSIS-KYPOSCOLIOSIS,

IDIOPATHIC DIFFUSE CERVICALGIA,

COGNITIVE DISORDER

EDEMA [LEG]

RENAL INSUFFICIENCY [KIDNEY]

FIBROMYALGIA

DIFFUSE LUMBAGO,

COPAL TUNNEL, ARTHRITIS,

ERBYS PALSY LEFT SIDE,

DAMAGE ROTATOR CUP RIGHT SHOULDER

DEALING WITH NOT BEING ABLE TO ENJOY A

PHYSICALLY, SPIRITUALLY AND A HEALTHY LIFE

EXPERIENCE IN JESUS.

MY YES TO CHRIST HOLDS ALL

MY UPS

DOWNS

RIGHT

WRONG

MY TRUTH

LIES

SUCCESS

FAILURES

HOPES

FAITH

DREAMS

DARKNESS

DEALING WITH

MY WHO

WHAT

WHEN

WHERE

HOW

WHY

MY REASON

PURPOSE

TRUST

BEING DIS-OBEDIENT TO HIS WORD,

AND DEALING WITH LIFE'S ISSUE.

HOW CAN I PLEASE GOD?

FEELING DEFEATED

NO HOPE IN SIGHT

UNABLE TO SUPPORT MY FAMILY AS BEFORE

BEING USELESS, BEING HALF A MAN,

TRYING TO UNDERSTAND WHAT GOD ALLOWS.

HAVING A RELATIONSHIP WITH 'GOD'

BELIEVING WHAT GOD SAYS AND REBUKING THE SINS

THAT'S COMMON TO MY FLESH.

NOT REAPING THE BENEFITS OF GODS PROMISES

WHEN EVERYTHING SEEMS TO BE

GOING IN THE WRONG DIRECTION.

WHAT ELSE TO DO?

NOTHING POSITIVE IS BEING PRODUCE

REJECTION

DISAPPOINTMENT

HOLDING ON TO WHAT LITTLE FAITH IS LEFT, IF ANY.

WAITING ON GOD WHILE THINGS GETS WORST.

HAVING THE SPIRITUAL WARFARE UNLEASH ON EVERY

ATTEMPT TO PROVIDE,

BEING RESPONSIBLE

TO ASSIST FAMILY AND OTHERS,

NOT GIVING UP ON ONE SELF

TRYING TO BE CONSISTENT IN

THE THINGS OF GOD,

BUT BEING OVERWHELMED IN THE

HARDSHIP OF MY TRIALS-TRIBULATIONS.

CHOOSING JESUS

AND DEPENDING ON HIM ONLY.

JUST BELIEVING HIS WORD;

THE TRUTH.

IN SPITE OF MY SUFFERING-N-AFFLICTION,

THE THINGS I PUT MY HANDS TO DO FOR SPIRITUAL GAINS

AS WELL AS NATURAL GAIN AND BEING BLESS PROSPERING.

BEING ANGRY WITH GOD FOR NOT BLESSING ME AND MINE.

THE ENEMIES ATTACKS ON MY CHILDREN BECAUSE I WAS NOT ABLE TO

PROVIDE FOR THEM.

I WAS HAVING A "JOB" EXPERIENCE IN THIS TIME-N-AGE.

WORN OUT

BROKEN

TIRED

WEAK

TORN

BEATEN

NO HELP FROM LIFE.

MIND, BODY, SOUL, EMPTY,

THINKING WHAT AM I GOING TO DO NOW?

IS THIS THE END?

I CAME AS FAR AS I COULD GO.

AND THEN, AT THE END OF THE DAY, GOD,

YOU ARE STILL WITH ME.

HE WHO IS ABLE TO DO EXCEEDING, ABUNDANTLY

ABOVE ALL I CAN ASK OR THINK OF, IS STILL WITH ME,

THOUGH TRAILS MAY COME ON EVERY SIDE,

THE HOLY SPIRIT IS STILL PRESSING ME FORWARD.

LORD YOU STILL REIGN,

THE GREAT "I AM THAT I AM."

THANK YOU LORD FOR EVERYTHING.

YOUR FRIEND,

RAY ANTHONY ROBINSON

12:20 AM 3/6/2013

MY TRUTH, SPIRIT AND HONESTY

[EL-ELYON] THE MOST HIGH GOD

HOW CAN I FIND YOU

SEE YOU

HEAR YOU

EMBRACE YOU

HOLD ON TO YOU

IN MY TROUBLES?

THE LIFE ISSUES ARE HEAVY DAY BY DAY.

I HAVE BRIGHT SKIES, YET DARKNESS RULES

MY SURROUNDINGS.

RAINY DAYS ARE PAINFUL DEEP WITH IN MY BONES

MY HEART IS COVERED IN GRIEF AND DESPAIR

MY EYES OPEN WIDE YET I CANNOT SEE.

THROUGH THE MIST OF MY HOPELESSNESS

I FIGHT WITH THE DISTINCTION OF MY SELF WORTH.

I HAVE BEEN HIDDEN FROM YOUR PROMISES.

JUST ANOTHER EMPTY PERIOD IN TIME.

MY NIGHTS ARE DRY.

MY MORNINGS ARE CHAPPED WITH

MY BURDENS OF YESTERDAY.

MY SONGS FOR HELP IS MUFFLED BY WEAKNESS.

MY SPIRIT IS FILLED WITH EMPTINESS.

HOW LONG MUST I SUCCUMB THESE

WEIGHTS OF SPIRITUAL WARFARE?

WITH IN ME DOES NOT LEAP AS THE GAZELLE,

NOR DASHES AS THE CHEETAH,

I AM STAGNANT.

NOTHING HAS DEVELOPED BUT HARDSHIPS.

ONE AFTER ANOTHER.

STILL I CHOOSE NOT TO SLIP BACK INTO THE DARKNESS

OF MY NOTHINGNESS,

NOT LOOKING FORWARD TO SEE TOMORROW.

I WAS TRYING TOO FIND PEACE IN COCAINE

OVERDOSE ON PAIN PILLS,

BEER,

WINE,

WHISKEY,

BOURBON,

PAUL MASON,

GRAY GOOSE,

SEAGRAM,

TANGAREY,

GIN,

SCOTCH,

MOONSHINE,

HENESSEY,

UPPERS,

WEED,

MONEY-N-WOMEN.

ANYTHING THAT WILL GIVE ME A HIGH AND PLEASURE

IS WHAT I DID.

BUT WITH THE PROMISES OF GOD.

THE HOPE. JOY, PEACE.

THE FINANCIAL FAVORS

THE BLESSINGS, DELIVERANCE'S

THE HEALING'S, FULFILMENTS

THE MIRACLES, GRACE, TRUST

THE BELIEFS,

FAITH

THE LOVE OF JESUS AND

ALL MY CHANGES FOR

ALL THE SPIRITUAL BENEFITS, I WILL MAKE IT OUT.

I PRAYED, LORD GOD, FATHER OF US ALL,

I AM GREATLY IN NEED OF THEM ALL.

I PLEAD MY CASE BEFORE YOU IN MY BROKENNESS,

AND YOU CAME TO MY RESCUE.

YOU RESTORED ME AND LIFT ME UP.

LORD, GIVE MY HEART THE DESIRES TO COMPLETE PURPOSE

IN MY LIFE FOR YOUR GLORY.

THROUGH ALL MY INCONVENIENCE THERE'S

STILL PRAISE, STILL WORSHIP.

FOR YOU ARE WORTHY OF ALL HONORS AND ALL GLORY.

MY SPIRIT BELONGS TO YOU ONLY

ALWAYS YOU, ALL MIGHTY GOD, AND NO OTHER.

8:25 AM 2/20/2013   RAY ANTHONY ROBINSON

Spiritual-Natural Moments

[ELOAH] THE ONE GOD

I understand we deal with earthy moments,

fleshly moments, human moments, historical moments.

All these and more moments

are nothing compared to the one moment of

His Birth

His growth

His Assignments

His Death

His Resurrection.

JESUS' life was filled with great historic moments.

My greatest moment was

JESUS Dying On The Cross For Me.

I Did for the Most part put me first, Him second.

No Man will ever be above GOD.

No Law,

No Creed,

No Religion,

No Amendment,

No Article,

No Flag,

No Man made inventions.

Nothing seeks precedence over his ways,

His Will,

His Commandments,

His Promises,

His Covenants,

His Glory,

His Holiness,

His Righteousness.

I should and always will be grateful to GOD.

I was dying from my lack of his knowledge

Yet he gave me a way out.

He said "If I will humble myself and seek his face

in prayer and

turn from my wicked ways;

Then He will hear from Heaven, and will forgive my

Sins, and Will Heal my Land".

He can see me headed wrongly but steered me in the right direction.

Why am I so special that he would do this just for me?

His Own Creation,

His Own Seed,

His Own Harvest,

His Own Likeness,

tainted, spoiled, corrupted.

Yet He took His time to separate the good part of me from the bad.

The good He put in the barn, The bad He put in the fire.

When I try to build my city of Babylon,

He confounds my mindset.

GOD in His Will—

allowed the devourer to take place,

But deliver me from the evil one.

I am learning what GOD is telling me to do,

He's not a Tyrant or a Dictator.

In all that I went through and will go through I came to the knowledge that

HE IS The ALFA and The OMEGA,

The Beginning and The End,

The Master, Ruler,

The Giver of life,

The Awesome ONE,

The Excellent Majesty,

The Powerful ONE,

The Holy ONE,

The Righteous ONE,

The Sovereign ONE,

The Merciful ONE,

The Faithful ONE,

The Omnipresent God,

The Omnipotent God,

The Omniscient God,

The God Over All,

The King of Kings,

The Lord of Lords,

The Great I AM THAT I AM,

The Good and Great Our Father.

I had forgotten and rejected the covering of God.

Exposed myself to be engulfed by destruction of all kind of sins

that is of the world.

What would life be like if I lived accordingly to the will of god?

Can I????.

"EMBRACE HIS GODLY MOMENTS"

Ray Anthony Robinson   Dec.18, 2012

My Name Is In The Lambs Book Of Life

[JEHOVAH-SHAMMAH] THE LORD IS THERE

We are always signing something,

but

What About His Book Of Life?

Sign here and here and there

Ok, here's your pay check.

Please sign on the bottom and I'll get your room key.

Sign on the dotted line and go to the left then right.

Sign these forms and we'll be with you in a moment.

Sign here for our consent to begin.

Sign here to receive ownership of.

Sign here for your membership.

Sign here for your approval.

Sign this get well, anniversary, birthday or congratulations card.

We sign our name on what we're asked

to sign our name on.

We will sign our life away to almost anything that this world presents to us,

when in truth it's a lie because of the fine prints.

If your name is not signed in the Lambs' book of life,

You won't be eligible for the process,

Or protection to receive eternal life.

But I know a man called

Jesus,

Who have signed my name

For all Eternity

In His Will

His Ways

His Commandments

His Covenant

His Promises

His Truth

His Death

His Resurrection

His life

His Coming back again.

MY name he signed with a 100 percent

Warranty.

That's Guaranteed

In His book.

He forgave my sins

Transgressions

Iniquities.

He signed My name,

My eternal resting place,

My Mansion,

Even My Departure is in his

Book of life.

Where no Man can Erase

My Name.

Jesus Signed My Name Just For Me,

No Identification

No Contract

No Credit Check

No Finger Prints

No Retina Eye Scan

No DNA

No Blood Test

No Physical Exam

No Waiting

No Take a Number

No I'll be with you in a moment.

My Name is Written in the

Lambs Book Of Life. Amen Amen Amen . . .

12:36 AM 9/27/2013

November 14, 2012

RAY ANTHONY ROBINSON

I AM LOOKING FOR A MAN

[JEHOVAH—SHALOM] THE LORD OUR PEACE

GREETING AND PEACE MY

SISTERS AND BROTHERS

DO YOU KNOW WHERE I CAN FIND THIS MAN EVERYONE

IS TALKING ABOUT?

I'VE NEVER SEEN THIS MAN

THAT'S SO SPECIAL TO THE WORLD.

PEOPLE ARE COMING FROM ALL OVER JUST TO HEAR AND SEE HIM.

WHO IS HE?

NEVER HAVE I HEARD SO MUCH ABOUT A MARE MORTAL.

HE MUST BE A WIZARD OR A GREAT MAGICIAN.

FOR ONE MAN TO HAVE SO MUCH FAME IS UN-HEARD OF.

HIS NAME IS PREACHED TO PEOPLE ABOUT SALVATION,

HIS DYING AND RESURRECTION.

HE HAS HEALED THE SICK, RAISED THE DEAD, AND OPEN BLINDED EYES.

HIS WORDS CAPTURES THE HEARTS OF MEN,

THE LEAST AND THE BEST OF THEM,

KINGS,

QUEENS,

DIPLOMATS,

RULERS,

PRINCES,

WISE MEN,

POOR MEN

WHOLE AND CRIPPLE MEN,

DEMON POSSESSED MEN,

EVEN MEN WHO CANNOT HEAR NOR SEE HIM,

EVEN THE DEAD.

I DO NOT KNOW OF SUCH A MORTAL.

HE MUST BE A WISE PHILOSOPHER.

I GUESS HE KNOWS HOW TO CONFUSE THEIR MINDS.

IT IS FASCINATING THAT SO MANY PEOPLE CAN BE

MISLEAD AT ONE TIME OR ANOTHER.

I WOULD LIKE TO SEE AND HEAR

THIS MAN OF SUCH GREATNESS, FOR MYSELF.

HE'S NOT RICH. HE HAS NO MONEY

FOR LODGING OR FOOD.

HE MUST ASK THE PEOPLE AND THEY GIVE HIM

OUT OF THE KINDNESS OF THEIR HEARTS

I WILL LEARN OF HIM,

FIND OUT WHAT MAGIC OR TRICKERY HE USE TO

OVERCOME THESE PEOPLE.

I DON'T KNOW WHERE HE'S FROM BUT

HE'S TRAVEL A GREAT DISTANCE WITHOUT ROAD TRANSPORTATION;

THE MANY PLACES HE'S BEEN

JERICHO,	BETHLEHEM	KORAZIN
CANA,	MT. TABOR	MAGDALA
JERUSALEM	KHERSA	GOLGOTHA
EMMAUS	TYRE	NAZARETH
PHILIPPI	CAESAREA	CAPERNAUM
BETHSAIDA	SAMARIA	BETHANY
	JORDAN,	

EVEN HIS WORDS WERE AT MANY MORE PLACES BEFORE HIM.

I WOULD LIKE TO MEET THIS MAN.

THE STORIES TOLD OF HIM INTEREST ME EVEN TO MY SOUL

AND SPIRIT.

HAVE YOU SEEN OR HEARD OF HIS WHERE ABOUT'S MY

FRIEND? IF SO PLEASE DIRECT ME TO HIS PATH.

RAY ANTHONY ROBINSON   JANURARY 3, 2013

If You Will Only, Just Trust Me

Only—[no one else. nothing more; exclusively; totally]

Just—[merely; simply; impartial; accurate; equal; righteous]

Jesus said to me,

RAY ANTHONY ROBINSON

"Can I just tell you of all the many wonderful and marvelous things

I will do for you"?

If you will only, just trust Me and cast all your cares upon ME.

I know all about your struggles

I know all about your sins

I know all things

I see all things

I hear all things

I created all things

All things belong to me, even you.

If you will only just trust ME

I Will make a way.

I Will guide you until the day is done.

I Will be a lamp post to your feet and a light to your pathway.

I Am The Alfa and The Omega,

I Am The Beginning and The End.

I Am Omnipotence

I Am Omniscience

I Am Omnipresent

No there is none like ME

No there is none righteous than ME

No there is none sovereign than ME

No there is none greater than ME

No there is none powerful than ME

No there is none worthier than ME

No there is none mightier than ME

No there is none holier than ME

No there is none compared unto ME

You can look high

look low

look to the east

look to the west

look to the south

look to the north

look near

look far

look on land

look in the seas

look on top of the high mountains

look in the lowest valley

There is none found like ME.

I AM THAT I AM.

I will deliver you.

I have all power and authority.

I can re-fix it

I've already solved it

I know how to work it out for your good.

What I have I will gladly give unto you.

I know how hard it is.

I know how hard it's going to be.

If you would have faith the size of a mustard seed,

I will bless you

I will heal you

I will favor you

I will restore you

I will save you

I will remove all your iniquities

I will give you freedom

I will fight all your battles.

For I Am The Almighty God.

My Name is Righteous

My Name is Holy

My Name is Sovereign

My Name is Above Every Name.

If you will only, just trust ME

With all your might

I will full your barns

I will fill your storehouses

I will increase your faith

I will increase your belief

I will increase your spirit

I will increase your wealth

I will increase your health

I will increase your anointing,

Everything you put your hands to do

Every place your feet shall tread

That is good

That is pure

That is honest

That is just

I will rebuke the devour for your sake.

If you will only, just trust ME

I am not a man that I should lie nor

The son of man that I should repent of my word.

For my word will not return unto me void

I can manifest your impossible to possible

There is nothing too hard for ME

You have no sorrows I can't heal.

I've never failed you

I can't fail you

You are the apple of my eye

If you will cast all your burdens

All your tears

All your fears

All your pains

All your sickness

All your troubles, cast them on ME

I will make a way out of your no way

If you will only just trust ME.

If I did it once, believe in ME

That I will do it again

I am The God of your many chances

I've never lost faith in you

I will never leave you nor will I forsake you

even till the end of time.

I will be with you

In your troubles

In your heartache

In all that is against you

I will give you peace.

God said "I and only I swear this by My Own Name, all these promises".

If you will only, just trust ME,

I love you with MY Unconditional Agape love

and there is nothing you can do about it.

My Child, Hear my voice".

"If You Will Only Just Trust ME, Just Trust ME".

Then I responded, "Thank you Holy Spirit"

HALLELUJAH.

Ray Anthony Robinson   3:15 PM 5/23/2013

WHEN I WAS OUT OF HIS WILL

I WAS GIVEN THE FREEDOM TO CHOOSE

THE DIRECTION TO GO

THE PATH TO FOLLOW

THE ABILITY TO MAKE DECISIONS

THINK OR THOUGHT WHAT'S BEST FOR ME.

I REALIZE HOW WRONG I WAS, FOR GOD KNOWS WHAT'S BEST.

THE WORD IS AND WILL ALWAYS BE MY GUIDELINE

TO LIVE IN HIS COMPLETE

PERFECT

WAYS AND WILL.

SO NOW I HAVE BEFORE ME TWO

FREE WILL CHOICES TO CHOOSE FROM,

MAINLY

GOD OR MAMMON

FLESH OR SPIRIT

HELL OR HEAVEN

SIN OR HOLINESS

DEATH OR LIFE

WHAT'S RIGHT OR WHAT'S WRONG;

CHOOSE.

I CAN RESPOND TO LIFE'S ISSUES BY THINGS OF THE WORLD

OR

THE WORD OF GOD.

I WILL REAP WHAT I SOW IN THIS LIFE

AND

THE NEXT.

I KNOW THAT SATAN HAS NO POWERS

BUT

THE ONES I GIVE HIM,

BUT

I HAVE EVEN THE MORE POWER THAT GOD GIVES ME

TO DEFEAT,

DESTROY,

REBUKE,

OVERCOME,

EVEN

TO ATTACK THE ENEMY'S PLANS TO DESTROY ME.

I AM NOT STUCK

WITH MY WRONG CHOICES

ONLY IF I CHOOSE TO.

BECAUSE GOD DESIGNED IT SO THAT I WILL

HAVE A WAY OF ESCAPE

THE GODLY WAY OUT

[JESUS].

THAT CHOICE COMES FROM GODLY PRINCIPALS

THE WILL AND WAYS OF GOD

WHICH HAS MY HEALING

DELIVERANCE

SALVATION

TO BRING ME TO WHERE I BELONG

TOO HIMSELF.

MY PRAYER IS TO BE HEALED

TO BE WHOLE

TO BE ONE IN EACH OTHER

TO BE ONE IN CHRIST.

WHEN I SEEK THE KINGDOM OF GOD

ALL THESE THINGS ARE ADDED UNTO ME.

I MUST TAKE HEED THAT

IF I COME OUT OF THE WILL OF GOD,

JESUS TELLS ME I WILL SUFFER GREATLY.

IF I REFUSE JESUS IN MY HEART

I SHALL BE CUT OFF FROM MY INHERITANCE.

THE TEMPTATIONS OF THIS WORLD IS JUST THE TOOLS

TO KEEP ME FROM PRESSING MY WAY TO THE MARK

OF THE HIGHER CALLING.

I KNOW THE CONSEQUENCES BEHIND MY WAYS ARE NOT

EQUAL TO THE WILL AND WAYS OF THE FATHER.

GOD GAVE ME THE OPPORTUNITY TO BE TRUSTED

WITH MY SUFFERING AND MY AFFLICTIONS.

MY UNCOMFORTABLE POSITION.

MY PURGING OF MY SPIRIT TO HANDLE AND

KEEP THE MANY BLESSINGS HE GIVE TO ME SO THAT I

WILL NOT EXCHANGE IT FOR ANYTHING OF THIS WORLD.

"HALLELUJAH, I AM EXCITED ABOUT YOUR TURN FOR DELIVERANCE."

MY FATHER LOVES ME.

AS A HUMAN BEING, I HAVE ADAPTED TO THE

MY WAY OF LIVING, RATHER THAN

HIS WAY.

THE FATHER KNOWS ALL THE DEEP THINGS OF MY HEART.

NOTHING IS KEPT FROM THE FATHER

NOR HIDDEN FROM JESUS

NOR DISGUISED FROM THE HOLY GHOST.

FOR I

CHOOSE THIS DAY WHOM I WILL SERVE.

I' M GLAD I DID

AMEN.

RAY ANTHONY ROBINSON   7/1/2013—1:15 PM-4:22 PM

THE CAUSE OF SPACE BETWEEN GOD AND MAN

Adam-Eve

[Deception, weakness lies, disobedience, fear]

Cain-Abel

Jacob-Esau

Joseph-Brothers

[Conspiracy, lies, trickery, greed jealousy]

Moses—Aaron

Ark Of The Covenant

Mount Sinai

[Anger, sinful nature, rebellion, lust]

Saul-David

[Pride, disobedience, rebellion`]

[Fear, envy, hatred, jealousy, weakness]

In each period of these events, sin caused a damaging amount of space

between these Great Men and GOD.

To be repeated through out time until the

coming of the Messiah and it shall be no more.

They are the same sin causing A Space Between Me And God

That search and seek to destroy my relationship with the Father.

I matter to the father. I am Valuable to Him.

Sin which has numerous amount of categories that I displayed in these

Many Forms,

Disobedience,

Hatred,

Envy,

Rebellion,

Anger,

Deceptions, lies, Deceit,

Pride, Conspiracy, Complaining, Lust, Arrogance,

Bribery, Treachery, Puffing Up, Murder, Resentment, Stealing,

False Worshipping, And Wickedness.

And much more that has put an empty space between God and me.

Sin has its ways of manipulation,

Just a whisper or thought can determine my

relationship with God when weakness sets in.

I learned that sin has a

Financial, and Physical

Consequences. It will also cause relationships to have devastating consequences.

That which follows, is not rewarding.

I know right from wrong, still I let it deceive me and enlarge the

Space that was causing A Space of Emptiness,

Defeat,

Captivity,

Hopelessness and Death.

I'm doing every thing In my being,

In my might,

In my Spirit,

In the word of God,

To fight,

Hold on, Pray, Cry, Moan

Groan, Dance, Praise and Worship to God,

To be nearer to thee at all times,

Filling That Dreadful Space Between ME and The Father.

"LIVE TO BE WITH JESUS."

I'M OFF TO A GREAT START. AMEN.

Ray Anthony Robinson   1:34 PM 5/28/2013

JESUS

PLEASE BLESS MY CHILDREN, THEIR CHILDREN,

THEIR CHILDREN'S, CHILDREN.

JESUS

PLEASE BLESS THE LITTLE CHILDREN

ALL OVER THE WORLD

AS A CHILD I WAS ALWAYS GOING

IN THE WRONG DIRECTION.

IT WAS A STRUGGLE WHEN

I HAD NO FATHER IN THE HOME.

I PUT MY CHILDREN THROUGH THE SAME THING.

I DO REGRET IT.

I HAD TO LEARN THE HARD WAY SO DID THEY.

I WAS A SORRY AND PATHETIC EXCUSE OF A FATHER.

I LOVED ALL MY KIDS THE SAME IN SPIRIT AND HEART.

I JUST DID NOT FOLLOW THROUGH.

I MISS THE BEST PART OF THEIR LIVE'S AS WELL AS MY LIFE.

NOW THERE GROWN,

KIDS OF THEIR OWN,

AND

I PRAY ALL THE TIME

LORD PLEASE BLESS MY CHILDREN-N-GRANDCHILDREN.

I STAYED IN TOUCH WITH THEM.

I GAVE THEM FREELY, IF I DIDN'T HAVE I FOUND AWAY.

NOW THEY GIVE ME WITH NO HARSH WORDS

LORD PLEASE BLESS MY CHILDREN.

WE HAVE A SPIRITUAL RELATIONSHIP,

GOD DID ANSWER MY PRAYERS.

I PRAY THEY WILL CONTINUE TO SEEK JESUS

AND BE A BLESSING TO THEIR KIDS AND OTHER KIDS AND

TREAT THEM AS THEIR OWN,

BECAUSE

THEY ARE LOOKING FOR THEIR FATHERS.

I KNOW I WAS BLESSED AS A CHILD BY JESUS.

ALL THAT

I WENT THROUGH, HIS HAND NEVER LEFT ME,

NEVER. NO MATTER WHAT SIN

I GOT INTO, MADE, AND DID WRONG,

I FELT HIM IN ME.

I KNOW ABOUT HARDSHIP.

WHO NEEDED A FATHER IN HIS EYE SIGHT,

TO TOUCH,

TO HEAR HIS VOICE,

TO FEEL HIS PUNISHMENT,

TO RECEIVE HIS LOVE

TO PROTECT

TO TEACH

TO GUIDE.

I PRAY FOR THE LITTLE ONES. FATHERS GATHER THEM

TOGETHER IN UNITY

AND

PRAY OVER THEM IN JESUS' MIGHTY NAME.

GOD BLESS THE LITTLE CHILDREN ALL OVER THE WORLD.

AMEN.

RAY ANTHONY ROBINSON   DEC. 22, 2012

I'M NOT LETTING YOU GO UNTIL

[JEHOVAH-SHAPHAT] THE LORD IS JUDGE

GREATER IS HE THAT IS IN ME THAN HE

THAT IS IN THE WORLD

I AM SPIRITUALLY SAVED BY GRACE

I HAVE RECEIVED THE HOLY GHOST POWER

I AM ANOINTED BY YOU, CHRIST JESUS

I AM SAVED BY THE NAME OF JESUS

I AM REDEEMED BY THE BLOOD

I HAVE RECEIVED SALVATION

EVERYTHING CONCERNING ME IS BLESSED

EVERYTHING OF ME IS COVERED IN

THE BLOOD

I HAVE WITNESS MY BREAKTHROUGHS

I HAVE SEEK YE FIRST THE KINGDOM OF GOD

I HAVE OVERCOME MY SINS

I HAVE RECEIVED THE ANOINTING POWER OF

DISCIPLESHIP

I HAVE BECOME A TRUE BELIEVER OF THE

GOSPEL.

I HAVE OPEN THE DOOR OF MY HEART

TO YOU

I HAVE RENEWED MY MIND.

I AM TAKING THIS VERY SERIOUSLY TO HEART.

RAY ANTHONY ROBINSON   NOVEMBER 15, 2012

A MESSAGE TO ACKNOWLEDGE

WHEN THAT TIME IS COME

I AM GOING TO MOVE TO A BETTER HOME

MY MANSION

[JEHOVAH-ELYON] THE LORD MOST HIGH

THIS OLD BUILDING HAS STOOD UP AGAINST THE TIME OF

HEARTACHE

HEADACHE

PAIN

SHAME

ICY RAIN

WEATHERLY TEARS

SEASONED FEARS.

THIS OLD BUILDING, HAS BEEN THROUGH ABUSIVE WINDS,

FIERY DARTS BY NIGHT

ARROWS BY DAY

SINKING SAND

CONSPIRED PLANS

THIS OLD BUILDING WEAKEN WITH DISEASE IN MY WALLS,

RAFTERS,

LOFT,

BEAMS,

MY VERY FOUNDATION HEATED IN HIGH

TEMPERATURES OF LIFE.

MY HOUSE

MY HOUSE FILL WITH RUST

SPIDER WEBS

MOTHS

SQUEAKY THINGS

DUSTY EYES

LAUGHTER'S OF BROKENNESS THROUGH OUT THIS HOUSE

WITH MY CRIES

ALL THE LIFE'S ISSUES BEFORE I DIE.

MY HOUSE.

AND NOW THE LONGEVITY OF ITS USE

HAS COME TO AN EXPECTED END.

A PRICE PAID IN FULL

ON

EARTH AS IT IS IN HEAVEN.

NOW IT'S TIME TO MOVE IN MY NEW HOME.

A MANSION

NO MORTGAGES

NO RENT

NO FIXER UPPER

NO CONTRACT—PAPERS

NO TAXES

NO BANK LIEN

NO REPOSSESSION

DON'T NEED

NO MAINTENANCE

NOR MAN

NO PUTTING UP FOR COLLATERAL

FOR MY CHILDREN'S SINS

NO MORE WORRYING ABOUT OWNERSHIP

NO MORE [MORBID]-DISEASE

NO DEPRESSION

NO BEING SICKLY UN-HEALTHY, AILING.

I JUST MOVED INTO A BETTER HOME

NOT BUILD BY FLESH BUT BY SPIRIT.

MY REALTOR CAME AND ESCORTED ME IN MY NEW HOME

A MANSION

BRAND NEW KEYS

PASTEURIZED FIELDS

BEAUTIFUL LANDSCAPE

PERFECT LOCATION

RIGHTEOUSNESS OF SCENERY

GOLDEN HONEY AND MILK STREETS

CRYSTAL SEAS

ILLUMINATED SKIES

ALL THE DAY LONG

MAGNANIMOUS COMMUNITY

GLORIOUS COMPANIES

NEIGHBORS FROM MY YESTERYEARS

THE ONES WHO SAID

YES LORD, YES LORD, YES LORD,

TO JESUS.

I AM LIVING IN A BETTER HOME A MANSION

A MANSION NEXT TO MY ELDEST BROTHER,

WHO'S SEATED

ON THE THRONE, ON THE RIGHT HAND OF THE

FATHER.

ONE MAY ASK, HOW DO I GET TO YOUR HOUSE?

JUST FOLLOW THESE DIRECTIONS,

LOOK FOR THE SIGN OF TRUTH

GO IN HIS WAY

THEN TURN IN YOUR LIFE

THEN WALK IN HIS PATH

THEN GO STRAIGHT UP

MY ADDRESS IS

HEAVEN ETERNAL PLACE.

RAY ANTHONY ROBINSON—10:57 AM 2/21/2013

OUR FATHER . . . YOUR NAME . . . YOUR WORD . . . YOU ARE . . .

YOUR NAME IS HOLY

YOUR NAME IS RIGHTEOUS

YOUR NAME IS SOVEREIGN

YOUR NAME IS ABOVE ALL NAMES.

YOU ARE OMNIPRESENT

YOU ARE OMNISCIENT

YOU ARE OMNIPOTENT

YOU ARE JEHOVAH

YOU ARE THE SAME GOD YESTERDAY,

GOD TODAY AND

GOD FOREVER MORE

GLORY TO YOUR NAME.

YOU ARE THE ALFA AND THE OMEGA

YOU ARE THE BEGINNING AND THE END

YOU ARE THE CREATOR,

THE DESIGNER,

THE OWNER,

THE POTTER,

THE MANUFACTURER,

THE ARCHITECTURE OF ALL THINGS,

UP ABOVE

DOWN BELOW

TO THE LEFT

TO THE RIGHT

IN SEASON

OUT OF SEASON.

YOU ARE THE GOD OF ABRAHAM

GOD OF ISAAC

GOD OF JACOB

YOU ARE MY CLOUD BY DAY

MY FIRE BY NIGHT

YOU ARE MY HEALER

MY DELIVER

MY PROVIDER

YOU ARE THE WAY

THE TRUTH

THE LIFE

YOU ARE ALL MIGHTY

ALL POWERFUL

ALL WISE

ALL MAJESTY

YOU ARE GLORIOUS

WONDERFUL

AN AWESOME WONDER . . .

YOUR WORD IS POWERFUL LIKE A TWO EDGE SWORD

YOUR WORD IS MY PEACE,

MY VICTORY

MY SALVATION

YOUR WORD IS MY ARMOUR AGAINST THE DREADFUL DAYS,

AND THE WICKED NIGHTS OF THE EVIL ONES.

YOUR WORD IS A STRONG TOWER

MY WEAPON TO REBUKE THE ENEMY

YOUR WORD IS TRUTH

MY ETERNAL LIFE

MY TEACHER

YOUR WORD IS FAITHFUL

YOUR WORD IS RIGHTEOUSNESS

YOUR WORD IS THE FOUNDATION OF MY EXISTENCE

MY BREAD OF HEAVEN

YOUR WORD IS A MIGHTY BATTLE AX

A GUIDE THROUGH THE DAY UNTIL IT IS

DONE

YOUR WORD IS MY TOOLS TO BUILD A

RELATIONSHIP AND ACCEPT JESUS

THE CHRIST.

RAY ANTHONY ROBINSON   10:00PM—//—11:30 PM 8/22/2013

IN THE PRESENCE OF THE LORD

THERE IS

GLORY, HONOR, SALVATION,

DELIVERANCE, REPENTANCE, POWER

PEACE, JOY, LIFE, ALL COMFORT

HOPE, TRUTH, PURITY.

IN THE PRESENCE OF THE KING

THERE IS

STRENGTH, RESTORATION, SHELTER,

CITIZENSHIP, COURAGE, AUTHORITY

FAITHFULNESS, FREEDOM, FORGIVENESS

GODLINESS, HOLINESS.

IN THE PRESENCE OF YOUR MAJESTY

THERE IS

VIRTUE, WORSHIP, TRUST, SINCERITY

VICTORY, PRESEVERANCE, DOMINION,

PRAISE. RELATIONSHIP, LOVE, RESOLUTION

HUMILITY, JUSTICE, PRAYER, OWNERSHIP.

AND THEN THERE IS ME, IN HIS PRESENCE, [-your-name-]

RAY ANTHONY ROBINSON   12:08 PM 6/6/2013

MY JESUS

A MAN CAME INTO TOWN WITH A PECULIAR SPIRIT,

STRANGE

PERSONALITY.

THE WAY HE LOOKS,

SPEAKS,

WALKS.

THIS STRANGER IS NOT LIKE ANY OTHER MAN

I'VE SEEN IN MY LIFE.

HE CALLED ME BY NAME

AS IF HE KNOWN ME ALL MY LIFE.

I DON'T NO WHERE HE CAME

FROM, NOR WHERE HE GOES.

I'VE NEVER SEEN HIM AROUND.

BUT,

I AM BEING COMPELLED TO FOLLOW HIM.

I CAME TO THE JORDAN RIVER AND I LOOKED.

PEOPLE CAME FROM ALL <u>JUDEA,</u>

AND <u>JERUSALEM.</u>

<u>AND COMING UP FROM</u>

<u>THE WATER WAS THIS STRANGER,</u>

<u>A DOVE RESTED ON HIS</u>

<u>SHOULDER AND THE STRANGER LEFT.</u>

HE LATER CAME TO GALILEE AND SAID:

THE TIME IS FULFILLED AND THE KINGDOM OF GOD

IS AT HAND; REPENT YE

AND

BELIEVE THE GOSPEL.

IT FELT LIKE MY BODY WAS BEING SEPARATED WITHIN ME.

I SAW PEOPLE BEING HEALED,

DELIVERED FROM ALL OF

THEIR AFFLICTIONS.

NEVER BEFORE HAVE I WITNESS SUCH POWER

AND

AUTHORITY FROM SUCH A MAN AS HE.

MEN FOLLOWED HIM EVERY WHERE.

HE SPOKE WITH POWER,

HIS EYES SPOKE TO MY SPIRIT AND

MY HEART WAS FILLED

WITH PEACE AND JOY LIKE NEVER BEFORE.

I FELT NEW INSIDE MY BODY,

AND

STRENGTH FROM A SPIRIT

CAME OVER ME.

I STARTED CRYING AND BEGAN TO PRAY WANTING THIS

STRANGER TO BE MY LORD AND KING.

I MUST GO TO HIM IN WORSHIP AND PRAISE

I KNEW OF HIM AS

"JESUS, THE SON OF THE LIVING GOD."

AFTER MANY DAYS PAST

I SAW A CROWD,

AND

SOLDIERS AT CALVARY.

LOW AND BEHOLD TO MY EYES,

THEY CRUCIFIED HIM BETWEEN

TWO MEN.

HIS BODY WAS TORN TO PIECES,

BLOOD AND WATER CAME

OUT OF HIM FROM HIS SIDE BY THE SOLDIERS SPEAR.

THE EARTH SHOOK AND SEPARATED FROM

THE CROSS TO THE TEMPLE.

THEY CRUCIFIED HIM WITHOUT CAUSE.

I HAVE NEVER FELT

SUCH PAIN WITHIN MY WHOLE BEING BEFORE.

AFTER THREE DAYS WAS GONE BY,

HE AROSE FROM THE DEAD.

AND

I SAW HIM ASCENDING UP TO HEAVEN.

"MY JESUS"

RAY ANTHONY ROBINSON   1:08 PM 9/2/2013

MY FIRST TIME ON A SPEAKERS PROGRAM

SUBJECT

"THE BELT OF TRUTH"

&

"99 1/2 WON'T DO"

I REMEMBER MY FIRST TIME EVER BEING A MESSENGER.

THEY LOVED IT.

THEY GAVE MY WIFE LINDA AND I THE CHANCE TO

SEE WHERE WE ARE IN CHRIST.

THEY HIGHLY ENCOURAGED US AT

GETHSEMANE CATHEDRAL OF PRAISE.

BISHOP ROBERT GATHERS JR. PASTOR

MINISTER GWENDOLYN GATHERS. FIRST LADY

99 1/2 JUST WON'T DO

WHEN JESUS WAS CARRYING HIS CROSS

HE FELL

AND

SOMEONE HELPED HIM TO CARRY

THE CROSS TO CALVARY FOR YOU AND ME.

HE KNEW WHAT HE MUST DO FOR YOU AND ME.

WHAT I WILL EXPERIENCE IS A SEPARATION FROM SIN IN EXCHANGE

FOR SALVATION.

JESUS KNOWS THAT MY SPIRIT IS CALLING HIM.

HE WANTS ME TO PICK UP MY CROSS AND FOLLOW HIM

EVEN THOUGH IT MAY BE HARD.

BUT HE WILL BE WITH ME TO SEE ME THROUGH.

SOME PEOPLE ARE NOT YOUR FRIEND

EVERY TIME YOU GET AROUND THEM THE ATMOSPHERE

CHANGES.

YOU HAVE MIX FEELINGS,

WHAT TO DO,

WHAT TO SAY.

THEIR ONLY YOUR FRIEND WHEN YOU GOT SOMETHING.

WHEN I READ THE WORD

I BEGAN TO READ MY LIFE STORY.

I BEGAN TO SEE TRUTH IN SO CALL FRIENDS.

I'M LEARNING WHAT A FRIEND REALLY MEANS,

ONE WHO WILL DO ANY THING THAT'S RIGHT

FOR YOU.

EVERYTHING'S GOOD WHEN WE'RE ALL IN

THE SAME BARREL

THE SAME BOX,

THE SAME BOAT GOING NOWHERE . . .

BUT ONCE I GAVE MYSELF A CHANCE

TO KNOW THE WHOLE TRUTH

AND

NOTHING BUT THE GOSPEL TRUTH

MY WHOLE LIFE BEGAN TO CHANGE.

I'M FOLLOWING JESUS MY TRUE FRIEND,

TO PARADISE,

NOT THOSE SO CALL FAKE FRIENDS.

THAT TURNS ON YOU FOR WANTING

TO TALK AND BE ABOUT JESUS.

THEY DON'T WONT TO HEAR CLEAN UPLIFTING

GODLY, CONVERSATION.

JESUS WILL NOT TREAT ME LIKE THAT.

HE'S THE 99 1/2 AND I'M THE 1/2.

ONCE I FOLLOW HIM, I BECAME THE 100

SPIRITUALLY ACCEPTED FRIEND OF

JESUS . . .

HE IS VERY INTERESTED IN BEING MY ONE TRUE FRIEND.

IT IS HARD BUT HE HELPS ME TO MAKE IT THROUGH

AND

I WILL NOT WORRY ABOUT WHO'S MY TRUE

FRIENDS FOREVER.

6\29\2012.

RAY ANTHONY ROBINSON

[EL-SHADDAI] GOD WHO IS ALL SUFFICIENT,

THE ALMIGHTY

THE BELT OF TRUTH

GIVES ME A CLEAR UNDERSTANDING OF THE TRUTH,

THE WORDS OF GOD.

JESUS WANTS ME TO BE SANCTIFY BY THE WORD OF GOD

WHICH IS THE TRUTH.

I AM TO TEST THE SPIRITS IN MY LIFE AND HOLD ON TO THE TRUTH ONLY

BY

1] READING SCRIPTURAL TRUTH

2] LIVING IN OBEDIENCE

3] SHARING THE GOSPEL

4] TRUSTING IN JESUS THE CHRIST.

THE BELT OF TRUTH CAN PROTECT ME WHILE I'M BEING

ATTACK BY THE EVIL ONE BY DAY AND BY NIGHT.

THE BELT OF TRUTH IS CLEAVED TIGHTLY AROUND MY WAIST

IN MY DAILY LIVING IN CHRIST TIGHTLY HOLDING MY LIFE IN PLACE.

I MUST NOT TAKE IT OFF [STOP READING THE WORD] OR

I WILL BE VUINERABLE TO THE ISSUES OF MY LIFE.

THE BELT OF TRUTH IS HELPING ME TO

HEAR THE WORD OF GOD TEACHING ME HOW TO LIVE HOLY AND RIGHTEOUS.

TO BE WITHOUT THE BELT OF TRUTH,

[LEANING TO MY OWN UNDERSTANDING]

I WOULD NEED MY HANDS TO HOLD UP MY PANTS

BEING UNABLE TO MANUVER AGAINST THE ENEMY'S DECECPTIONS, LIES, AND TEMPTATION.

THE BELT OF TRUTH IS ESPECIALLY DESIGNED TO BE WORN BY

THOSE WHO ARE;

ABUSED

BEAT ON

BROKEN LEFT FOR DEAD

LONELY

WEAK

POVERTY STRICKEN

BLIND

HELPLESS

LOST

DEFEATED

BETRAYED

DISTRAUGHT,

EMOTIONALLY, MENTALLY, AND PHYSICALLY.

WEAR YOUR BELT OF TRUTH ALLWAYS SO YOU WILL NOT BE CAUGHT

WITH WEARING SAGGING DOWN PANTS.

[DON'T GET CAUGHT WITH YOUR PANTS DOWN]

WEAR YOUR BELT AND MAKE SURE IT IS TIGHTLY SECURED.

AMEN

MR. RAY ANTHONY ROBINSON SR.   6/21/2012

HE PRAYS FOR ME

[ADONAI-JEHOVAH-SABOATH] MASTER LORD OF HOST

HE PRAYS THAT I COME TO HIM BELIEVING

THAT HE IS

"THE GREAT I AM THAT I AM"

MY HEART, MIND, SOUL, MUST COME TO HIM

BELIEVING

HE IS ABLE TO DO EXCEEDING

ABUNDANTLY ABOVE ALL THAT

I CAN IMAGINE

OR ASK FOR ACCORDING TO

THE POWER THAT WORKETH IN ME.

HE'S PRAYING FOR ME.

JESUS PRAYS THAT I BECOME ONE WITH MYSELF

AND MY BROTHERS AND SISTERS

IN ORDER TO BECOME ONE WITH HIM.

MY ENEMIES ARE DEFEATED

LYING TONGUES ARE CONDEMED.

MY HEALING IS RESTORED

I'M FREE FROM SLAVERY OF MY FLESH

I'M STRONGER-WISER IN FAITH

I'M HEALTHY-WEALTHY IN STATURE

IN UNITY, IN FELLOWSHIP,

A BELIEVER OF THE GOSPEL TRUTH.

BEING ONE IN THEM COVERS AND JUSTIFIES

ME IN THESE MATTERS . . .

HE'S PRAYING FOR ME.

JESUS PRAYS THAT I'M MADE PERFECT

WHOLE, COMPLETE, A UNIT

WITH THE DESIRE AND PASSION TO

CHASE AFTER GOD AND NOT THE WORLD,

SEEKING THE FACE OF GOD ALWAYS.

TO LOVE ONE ANTOHER WITH THE LOVE OF CHRIST,

THAT I MAY KNOW THAT IT IS GOD THAT SENT HIS

ONLY BEGOTTEN SON; OUT OF LOVE; FOR ME.

HE'S PRAYING FOR ME.

JESUS PRAYS THAT I AM TO BE WITH HIM.

WHERE HE IS, I MAY BE ALSO.

HE WILL NOT LEAVE ME NOR FORSAKE ME.

NO MATTER WHERE I AM IN LIFE'S TESTS

LIFE'S ISSUES

TRAILS-TRIBULATION

TRESPASSES

TRANSGRESSION

ENIQUITIES

FAULTS-MISTAKE

OMISSION, COMMISSION

OF MY SINS,

HE'S PRAYING FOR ME.

TO BE ONE WITH EACH OTHER IN JESUS,

THEN JESUS AND I WILL BE ONE WITH THE FATHER.

AS HE'S PRAYING FOR ME,

I'LL PRAY FOR YOU,

ALL BELIEVERS AND NON BELIEVERS. AMEN

RAY ANTHONY ROBINSON   1:08 PM 2/15/2013

GODLY PRINCIPLES

HONESTY—TRUTH—HOPE

HONESTY

WAS SOMETHING I TOOK ADVANTAGE OF

FOR WORLDLY USE.

I LIED GOT CAUGHT, LIED MY WAY OUT

AND

BECAME, I THOUGHT, A REAL GOOD LIAR.

IT WAS CONVICTION THAT MADE ME FEEL BAD,

BECAUSE I KNEW I WAS LIYING.

THEN ALL KIND OF THINGS STARTED HAPPENING.

I COULD NOT FIGURE

OUT WHY PEOPLE STOP TALKING TO ME,

I WAS REJECTED,

PEOPLE DIDN'T WANT TO BE AROUND ME.

WHY I COULD'NT GET IT TOGATHER?

THEN IT CAME TO ME, "TELL THE TRUTH".

I LIED SO MUCH THE TRUTH SOUNED LIKE A LIE.

I TOOK A LIE DETECTOR TEST FOR A JOB,

I WAS SCARED OUT OF MY SKIN.

THEN I REMEMBER I WAS A GOOD LIAR, BUT I WAS

TO SCARED TO TELL THE TRUTH.

LORD PLEASE LET ME PASS THIS TEST.

I DID PASS THE LIE DETECTOR TEST,

HAPPIER THAN A HOMELESS MAN

ON A PULL OUT BED COUCH.

A LIAR LIKE ME PRAYING TO GOD FOR HELP.

WHEN I GOT THROUGH, I THROUGHT I WAS GOING TO JAIL.

A LESSON WELL TAUGHT. I DIDN'T GET THE JOB.

BUT I FOUND OUT THE TRUTH

WHY I DID'T GET THE JOB,

AS A CHARLESTON CITY POLICE OFFICER.

MY MOTHER AND FATHER WAS THE ONLY TWO

WHO PRAYED FOR ME.

THEY WERE AFFRAID FOR MY LIFE.

THEY TOLD GOD THE TRUTH OUT OF LOVE,

AND I TOLD THE TRUTH TO GET A JOB.

UP TO THIS DAY I CAN TELL THE TRUTH

AND

NOTHING BUT THE TRUTH,

SO HELP ME GOD.

BE HONEST AT HEART. I HAVE NO REASON TO LIE.

JOB DIDN'T HAVE A LIE DETECTOR TEST.

SO HE SWORE AN OATH IF HE HAS SIN AGAINST GOD,

THAT GREAT HARM FALLS UPON HIM.

THE ONLY WAY TO PROVE HIS INNOCENCE, WAS TO

JUST TELL THE TRUTH.

LYING LIPS ARE ABOMINATION TO THE LORD.

THE TRUTH BRINGS OUT THE HONESTY IN ME.

RAY ANTHONY ROBINSON   8:54 PM 10/23/2013

HOPE

I WAS HOPING FOR ALL THE WRONG THINGS

I HOPE SHE'S COMING BY HERSELF,

THEY GOT THE LIQOUR, BEER, WINE, THE POWDER

THEIR NOT GOING WITH ME

THEY DONT BE TO LONG IN CHURCH

THEY GET THE WINGWHAM BEAT OUT THEM

THEY DON'T NEVER COME BACK

THEY GET SICK, AND DIE. I HATE THAT SORRY DOG

THEY NEVER GET PAY

THAT'S GOOD FOR'EM

HER HUSBAND AIN'T HOME

I WAS HOPING FOR ALL THE WRONG REASONS

IN ALL MY SINS.

NOW I'M BEING TAUGHT HOW TO HOPE IN GOD.

I PUT MY HOPE IN GOD.

BECAUSE OF ALL MY WRONG DOINGS, AFFLICTIONS CAME.

I WAS RAGGED WHEN I GOT SAVED,

I LOOKED GOOD OUTSIDE BUT

FILTHLY,

ROTTEN,

DISFIGURED,

STINK,

CORRUPT

VIAL

UGLY INSIDE.

THE BEST DECISON I MADE IN MY ENTIRE LIFE,

WAS COMING TO JESUS.

I LEARNED HOW TO REALLY APPRECIATE

GOD

IN ALL MY AFFLICTIONS.

NO, IT DID NOT FELT GOOD AT ALL,

BUT WITH TIME-PATIENCE

CAME MY HEALING.

MY BROTHERS—SISTERS

TRUST GOD, HE WILL FORGIVE YOU

JUST BE HONEST, TRUST HIM AND HAVE HOPE.

HE WILL HELP YOU TO BE CONQUERS.

RAY ANTHONY ROBINSON   11:36 AM 10/26/2013

HUMILITY

BEING HUMILIATED, JESUS HUMBLED HIMSELF.

I GOT MAD AND WANTED TO FIGHT.

FEAR GRAB ME MOST OF THE TIME, IN THE FORM OF HUMILITY.

IF I DIDN'T HUMBLE MYSELF, I WOULD BE BEATEN DOWN LIKE A RUNAWAY SLAVE.

THE MORE I WAS HUMILIATED I LEARN TO ENDURE.

LOT'S OF TIME I WAS BEING TESTED.

BECAUSE IF I DIDN'T HAVE NO ROOM FOR

HUMILITY I WOULD BE CRUSHED OR DESTORYED.

I WAS ALLWAYS BEING PRIDEFUL ABOUT WHAT I

ACHIEVED. THAT WAS MORE IMPORTANT TO ME THAN MEEKNESS.

I'M LEARNING A LOT ABOUT HOW I SHOULD RESPOND.

IT IS AN UNCONTAINMENT OF

PEACE, JOY, HEART, LOVE,

IN MY HUMILITIES.

. I'M LEARNING TO LOVE IT. IT'S GREAT FOR MY SOUL.

I KNOW FOR SURE THAT HE WILL

REMEMBER

MY HUMBLE CRIES. AMEN

RAY ANTHONY ROBINSON   12:49 PM 10/26/2013

DECISIONS—DECISIONS—DECISION

SOMETIMES I GET STUCK WITH IT.

JESUS NEVER GOT STUCK WITH A DECISON CONCERNING ME,

GIVING ME THE RIGHT OPPORTUNITY

TO DECIDE MY LOVE

FOR HIM.

LEARNIG HOW TO MAKE GODLY DECISIONS.

TO SOW AND REAP SPIRITUALLY,

CHOOSING JESUS OVER THE WORLD.

WHEN I REPEATLY RESISTED HIS WILL,

HIS WAYS, I WAS BEING DECIEVED, DETERMINE AND STUBBORN,

IN REJECTING HIM.

I BECAME UNABLE TO CHANGE IN SPITE OF MY MANY CHANCES

TO MAKE THE RIGHT DECISIONS.

THE ANGEL OF THE LORD WHO WAS ASSIGNED TO ME

KEPT ME THROUGH MY SINS,

ABOMINATION, WICKEDNESS, DEATHS.

THANK YOU JESUS.

REVISIONING THE SINS I DID IN HIS EYE

HE LITERALLY STOPS ME FROM COMMITTING THEM.

THREE TAPS WITH HIS FINGERS ON MY RIGHT SHOULDER

CHANGED MY LIFE, AND CHRIST BECAME MY DECISION.

JAN. 11 2013   RAY ANTHONY ROBINSON

LORD JESUS SHOW UP AND SHOW OUT

[IMMANU-EL] GOD WITH US

I NEED YOU TO SHOW UP AND SHOW OUT

IN MY LIFE

GOALS

DESIRES, PLANS

SUCCESS, VICTORY

HOME, CHURCH

CHILDREN, FINANCE

HEALTH, SICKNESS

PAIN, STRUGGLES

ISSUSES OF LIFE, LACK, MORE THAN ENOUGH

TRIALS—TRIBULATIONS

FALLING DOWN, GETTING UP

PRESSING TOWARD THE MARK OF THE HIGH CALLING

IN MY SPIRIT, MY PRAYERS

MY CRY, MY PLEA FOR HELP

MY TRUTH, BREAKTHROUGHS

DELIVERANCE, SALVATION

PROSPERITY, AS MY SOUL PROSPERS.

THANK YOU JESUS,

HALLELUJAH, HALLELUJAH, HALLELUJAH . . .

I NEED YOU TO SHOW UP AND SHOW OUT IN

YOUR UNCONDITIONAL AGAPE LOVE

YOU'RE PROMISES

YOU'RE MERCY-GRACE

YOU'RE WORD OVER MY LIFE

YOU'RE PLANS FOR MY LIFE

IN MY SPIRITUAL WARFARE

IN MY MANY BATTLES

IN THE RENEWING OF MY MIND

IN MY WALK WITH JESUS

IN MY TALK WITH JESUS

IN MY SIGHT, IN MY YES

IN MY CONFESSION

IN THE ATTACK OF MY ENEMIES

IN MY LATTER DAYS

IN MY FORMER DAYS

IN THE BLOOD OF JESUS

IN MY DANCE

IN MY PRAISE

IN MY WORSHIP

IN MY CALLING.

I NEED YOU TO SHOW UP AND SHOW OUT WHEN I'M

BLESSING YOUR NAME

PRAISING YOUR NAME

WORSHIPPING YOUR NAME

SEEKING YOUR KINGDOM AND ALL YOUR RIGHTEOUSNESS

IN ALL YOUR GLORY

IN HEAVEN AS IT IS ON EARTH

IN ALL MY SINS.

IN MY VALLEY OF THE SHADOW OF DEATH

IN MY PATH WAY TO YOU

IN MY HEART

IN MY LYING DOWN

IN MY RISING UP

IN MY VALLEY OF DRY BONES . . .

I NEED YOU TO SHOW UP AND SHOW OUT

IN MY LIVING

IN MY DYING

IN MY DISOBEDIENCE—OBEDIENCE

TO YOUR WILL AND YOUR WAYS.

IN MY, GREATER IS HE THAT'S IN ME, THAN HE THAT'S IN THE WORLD,

IN MY WORRIES

MY WEAKNESS

MY POVERTY

MY ANOINTING

MY STINCH

MY FILTH

MY WRECHED FLESH

MY HUNGER

MY THIRST

MY SHELTER

MY BROKENNESS

MY ALL THAT'S WITHIN ME

SHOW UP AND SHOW OUT IN ALL MY DAYS,

SHOW UP AND SHOW OUT FOR ME YOUR CHILD

RAY ANTHONY ROBINSON,

THANK YOU JESUS. AMEN   4:33 AM 4/3/2013

[JEHOVAH]—YAHWEH, LORD, I AM,

THE SELF EXISTENCE ONE

WHERE WERE YOU???

WHEN they told his mother no room?

WHEN He was born KING in a manger

wrapped in the "finest and purest" of swaddling clothes.

WHEN By prophesy He was worshiped near and far.

WHEN wise men brought Him silver and gold, making Him surrounded

by the finest scenery created by 'GOD'.

WHEN they heard an seek out to destroy him with all the

other newborns.

WHEN they were looking for him with panic and fear and he's

in his fathers house.

WHEN He was sent to orientation for 40 days and nights

WHEN He got his first uniform (baptism)

WHEN He started his first job, for three years, with an excellent

work history, never late, never called in sick, always on time.

WHERE WERE YOU?

WHEN They accused him of lying on his application; false

information, offensive background check.

WHEN they conspired, betrayed and didn't know him.

WHEN they fired him after he told the truth in court.

WHEN after he gave them three of the best years of his life.

WHEN they strip him of all his good works, took away his

glorious presence an awards.

WHEN they escort him to HIS EMPLOYER, with his arms stretched out wide crying to THE OWNER.

ELI, ELI, WHY HAS THOU

FORSAKENED ME!

WHEN HE gave up everything of himself and did not uttered

a hateful word but words of appreciation.

WHEN He was hired 3 days later as

'KING OF KINGS'

'LORD OF LORDS'

'JUDGE OVER ALL JUDGES'

OVERSEER OVER ALL THINGS.

WHEN HE was given the power and the authority to hire and fire.

WHERE WERE YOU?

IN HIS MIND, HEART AND SPIRIT.

Ray Anthony Robinson   December 10, 2012

THE WASHBOARD STORY

I REMEMBER MY MOTHER

WASHING DIRTY CLOTHES

IN THE SINK OR WASH TUB WITH

HOT WATER

LYE SOAP

AND A

WASHBOARD.

SHE PUTS THE DIRTY CLOTHES IN

AND

BEGINS TO SCRUB THE LINEN AGAINST

THE RUFFLE PART OF THE WASHBOARD,

UP, DOWN, REPEATEDLY.

WHEN SHE GETS HER RHYTHM GOING

SHE GETS FUELED UP BY ALL THE DIRT

THAT IN THE GARMENTS

AND

HER POSTURE SHIFTS IN HUMMING SPIRITUAL SONGS.

SO SHE CAN COMPLETLY GET ALL THE DIRT OUT,

SHE HAND RANG THE DIRTY WATER OUT

AND

PUT THE CLOTHS IN THE CLEAR CLEAN WATER

LET SOAK

AND

START OVER AGAIN

WITH THE NEXT PIECES OF DIRTY CLOTHES.

WHEN SHE GETS ENOUGH FOR THE RINSE

SHE NOW SHIFTS INTO ANOTHER POSTURE

SINGING OUT LOUD

WITH HER FINGERS SPREAD OPEN

PUSHING THE CLOTHES FROM TOP TO BOTTOM

OR WITH

THE CLOTHES IN HER CLOSED FIST RUBBING

THE SOAP OUT SEAVERAL TIMES UNTIL

SHE KNOWS THAT'S ENOUGH.

SHE GRABS ONE OR TWO PEICES AND SQUEEZE FROM

THE TOP TO BOTTOM

RING OUT

FOLD IT

LAY IT DOWN.

SHE PUTS MORE DIRTY CLOTHES IN

LET IT SOAK UNTIL SHE FINISH HANGING OUT

THE CLEAN CLOTHES TO DRY.

SHE STARTS ON THE NEXT BATCH

WITH THE SAME TECHNIQUE UNTIL SHE'S COMPLETELY DONE.

THAT'S HOW MY LIFE WAS WASHED WHEN I WAS DIRTY

AND

LIVED FILTHY DIRTY.

I SAW MYSELF, MY LIFE,

DIRTY, FILTHY IN NEED OF WASHING.

I SAW THE PREPERATION FOR MY

CLEANSING.

I SAW THE POSTURE SIN SHIFTED

ME INTO NEEDING TO BE WASHED.

I FELT THE RUBBING OUT OF SIN

FROM MY FLESH.

I FELT THE SQUEEZING OF PRESSURE

FROM DEPRESSION, STRESS, STRIFE, SICKNESS,

LEAVING MY SPIRIT.

I SAW MYSELF IN JESUS WASHTUB

TAKING A BATH.

THE DIRTY FILTH IS MY SINS,

JESUS IS MY MOTHER

AND

THE WASHBOARD IS MY CROSS.

I'M BEING CLEANSED

RAY ANTHONY ROBINSON   5/23/13

WHY???

[JEHOVAH-ELOHIM-SABOATH] THE GOD OF HOST

WHY DID YOU BIRTH ME, SO YOU CAN KILL ME?

WHY ME?

WHY HOLD AND KISS ME, SO YOU CAN YELL AND CURSE ME OUT

WHY ME?

WHY SMILE AND CELEBRATE ME, SO YOU CAN CALL ME NAMES AND DISHONOR ME?

WHY ME?

WHY FEED, CLOTHES AND SHELTER ME, SO YOU CAN ACCOMMODATE YOUR SELF?

WHY ME?

WHY DO YOU WANT TO BE AROUND ME, SO YOU CAN EXPLOIT ME.?

WHY ME?

WHY CALL MY NAME, SO YOU CAN FORGET ME DAYS, HOURS, WEEKS, MONTHS AT A TIME

WHY ME?

WHY DO YOU SAY YOU LOVE ME, SO I CAN FEEL OR SAY THAT I HAVE A MOTHER?

WHY ME?

WHY ARE YOU GIVING ME THINGS AND BEING NICE TO ME, SO YOU CAN MOLEST ME.

WHY ME?

WHY DID YOU SET A TRAP FOR ME? SO YOU CAN PROSTITUTE ME TO STRANGERS?

WHY ME?

IF THIS IS THE CASE KNOWINGLY OR UNKNOWINGLY,

LORD PLEASE SPEARE ME THOSE EXPEREINCES.

DECEMBER 16, 2012 AKA G-DADDY RAY A. ROBINSON

BIBLICAL—INSTRUCTIONS—BEFORE—LEAVING—EARTH,

[JEHOVAH-KANNA] THE LORD WHO IS JEALOUS

MY MANUAL,

GUIDE LINE,

FORMAT,

FOUNDATION OF STRUCTURE

HOLY,

SPIRITUAL,

GODLY LIVING,

HOW TO PUT THE PEACES TOGATHER

IN ORDER

FOR LIFE TO FUNCTION.

ALL I NEED TO DO

IS TO JUST FOLLOW INSTRUCTION.

I WILL NOT ADD NOR TAKE AWAY FROM MY INSTRUCTION

NOR LEAN TO MY OWN UNDERSTANDING.

THE FINISHED PRODUCT IS

THE BUILDING AND COMPLETION

OF

HEARING THE WORD OF GOD.

WHERE I ATTEND CHURCH OUR THEME IS

"WHERE HEALING BEGINS AND IS COMPLETED",

BUT ONLY

WHEN I FOLLOWED GODS INSTRUCTIONS FOR MY LIFE

ACCORDING TO HIS WORD, AND

AT A LEVEL OF OBEDIENCE.

THE FINISHED PRODUCT OF

MY HURT-PAIN—IT'S FINISHED

SINFULL NATURE

TEARS

FEARS

POVERTY

MY SUFFERING—IT'S FINISHED

INFIRMITIES

WORRIES

STRUGGLES

DEPRESSION

MY DRUG HABIT—IT'S FINISHED

WHORING

DRINKING PROBLEM

SATAN HAVING HIS WAY IN ME.

IT'S FINISHED.

SAINTS READ THE B.I.B.L.E., . . . AMEN

9:00 AM 2/13/2013 RAY ROBINSON

??? WHERE'S THE TRUTH

[ADONAI] THE MASTER, THE OWNER—RULER OF ALL

IS IT LOST?

IS IT HIDDEN?

IS IT WAITING TO BE FOUND?

IS IT COVERED UP.?

IS IT IN THE WIND GOING WHERE EVER

IT CHOOSE TO BLOW

OR THE WAVES IN THE OCEAN TOSSED

TO AND FRO?

IS IT BEING EXSPOSED FOR ME TO VIEW?

DID THE TRUTH EVER EXSISTED?

IS IT ON TOP OF THE HIGHEST MOUNTAIN?

IS IT IN MY MOUTH, MY HEART

MY SOUL, MY SPIRIT?

WHAT I DO THAT'S RIGHT?

WHERE'S THE TRUTH?

THE TRUTH WAS IN A TOMB,

THE GOSPEL TRUTH

RAISED 3 DAYS LATER,

PRIVATELY SHOWN AND

LIFTED HIGH TO BE WITNESS BY ALL

MY LIES,

RETURNED FROM WHERE IT CAME.

THE TRUTH THAT HAVE THE POWER

TO SET ME FREE INDEED . . .

RAY ANTHONY ROBINSON NOV.20, 2012

LORD, AM I IN YOUR PERFECT WILL?

[JEHOVAH-SABOATH] THE LORD OF HOSTS

I TRY NOT TO QUESTION YOUR SUPERIORITY

WHAT THINGS YOU HAVE FOR ME,

TO SAY,

TO DO,

WHERE TO GO,

WHO TO MEET AND GREET.

WHY AM I NOT BLESSED LIKE YOU SAY I'M BLESSED?

THAT WHICH WAS SPOKEN IN MY LIFE,

YOU'RE PROMISES I'VE RECEIVED IN MY SPIRIT.

I FEEL I'M BEING STRIP OF EVERYTHING YOU SAID

I CAN HAVE, I CAN BE, AND I CAN ACHIEVE

I N YOUR NAME, JESUS

MY FAITH IS LITTLE, NOT ENOUGH TO SEE WHAT

IS NOT THERE THAT SHOULD BE.

MY TRUST IS SHAKY, MY BELIEF IS SHADY.

I AM HAVING A HARD TIME

WITH MY TRIALS AND TRIBULATIONS LIKE NEVER BEFORE.

I PUT MY HANDS TO THE PLOW

AND

NOTHING GOOD HAPPENS,

NOTHING POSITIVE,

PRODUCTIVE BECOMES OF IT.

LORD AM I IN YOUR PERFECT WILL?

PLEASE FORGIVE ME OF MY HUMAN NATURE,

TOWARDS YOUR SOVEREIGNTY.

I KNOW WHO YOU ARE,

WHAT YOU ARE,

WHERE YOU ARE.

LORD I'M STANDING IN THE NEED OF HEALING,

FINANCIAL,

SPIRITUAL BREAK THROUGHS.

TRULY I DON'T UNDERSTAND THESE ATTACKS ON MY

RESPONSIBILITIES.

I FEEL SO BOUND, I CAN EVEN SEE MY BLINDNESS.

THE CONCEPT OF GODS PROMISE

IN MY LIFE IS

BURDENS OF DISPAIR.

I NEED A WAY OUT OF MY TROUBLESOMES DAYS.

AM I TO HOLD YOU RESPONSIBLE

FOR EVERY PROMISE YOU MADE TO ME

IF I RECEIVE THE LORD JESUS IN MY HEART . . .

LORD I LOOK FOR YOUR HELP,

PRAYING THAT YOU WILL HEAR AND ANSWER ME

BUT

I GUESS I'M NOT BEING OBEDIENT, NOR FAITHFUL TO YOU.

I KEEP TRYING TO WORK IT OUT IN PRAYER,

TRUST, FAITH, AND BELIEF,

IN YOUR WORD.

LORD I EVEN TRY TO WORK IT OUT IN MY OWN STRENGTH.

MY MIND WONDERS IN CONFUSION,

MY HEART SINKS IN DEFEAT.

LORD AM I IN YOUR PERFECT WILL?

DO I MEAN ANYTHING TO YOU?

MY HURT

MY PAIN,

MY REJECTION,

MY FEARS,

MY SETBACKS,

MY FAILURES,

MY FAULTS,

MY TEARS,

MY HATERS,

MY BETRAYERS,

MY BROKENESS,

MY LOVE . . .

WHAT HAVE I DONE TO HURT YOU SO GREIVOUSLY?

ONLY YOU KNOW WHAT I FAIL TO KNOW

PLEASE FATHER IN HEAVEN I BEG FOR

MERCY, GRACE AND FORGIVNESS.

IN MY LACK,

WEAKNESS,

UNBELIEF,

INSECURITY,

MY SOUL AND SPIRIT.

FATHER GOD, ALLMIGHTY GOD YOU ARE MY ONE AND ONLY:

EMMANUEL: MY LORD, BLESS YOUR HOLY NAME.

THAT I MAY BE IN YOUR PERFECT WILL . . . AMEN

12-6-2012

RAY ANTHONY ROBINSON

JESUS WILL REACH WAY DOWN AND LIFT ME UP

[EL-GIBBOR] THE GREAT GOD

I SAW IN THE SPIRIT

THE HAND OF GOD COMING DOWN FROM HEAVEN

INTO THE EARTH

REACHING WAY DOWN TO LIFT ME

AND OTHERS LIKE ME UP . . .

I PAUSED IN AWE OF HIS LOVE,

COMPASSION

POWER

AND HIS MERCY . . .

I BEGAN TO REALIZE THE POWER OF HIS LOVE FOR ME

HE WILL NOT LEAVE ME

NOR WILL HE FORSAKE ME.

[HE REACHED THROUGH TIME AND SPACE.]

HE KNEW ME BEFORE I EVER EXISTED

EVEN BEFORE TIME.

HE REACH DOWN TO

SAVE ME.

[HE REACHED THROUGH THE HEAVENLY AND EARTHLY CLOUDS]

JESUS REACHING WAY DOWN

LIFTING ME UP OUT OF MY DEPRESSION

OUT OF MY ADDICTIONS

OUT OF MY TROUBLED MIND

OUT OF MY WICKEDNESS

OUT OF MY FILTH

OUT OF MY DEFEATS

OUT OF MY POVERTY

OUT OF MY FLESH

OUT OF MY IDOLATRY

JESUS REACH WAY DOWN AND LIFT ME UP

OUT OF MY SINS

AND THERE WERE MANY . . .

[HE REACHED THROUGH ALL MY IMPOSSIBILITIES]

HE DID IT JUST FOR ME . . .

BECAUSE WHEN HE STARTED

PASSING OUT BLESSING

HE WANTED TO MAKE SURE I RECEIVED MY PORTION,

MINE.

OUR RELATIONSHIP STARTED

WHEN HE GAVE UP THE GHOST ON THE CROSS WHERE

THERE WAS ROOM AT THE CROSS RESERVED JUST FOR ME.

HE REACHED WAY DOWN AND LIFTED

ME UP IN HIS WITNESS PROTECTIVE CUSTODY.

HE GAVE ME RIGHTEOUSNESS,

FAITH

REST

REVIVAL

SALVATION

CONFIDENCE

FORGIVENESS

HOPE.

HE GAVE ME ANOTHER CHANCE.

SO I GAVE HIM ME WHEN I LIFTED UP MY HANDS,

HIS PRAISE

HIS WORSHIP

HIS HONOR

MY ALL, FOR HIS GLORY.

IN THE SPIRIT I SAW THE HANDS OF GOD

REACHING WAY DOWN IN THE EARTH LIFTING US UP.

6:15 AM 3/21/2013   RAY ANTHONY ROBINSON

ATTACK

[ELOHIYM—MIGHTY ONE]

I HAVE THE WORD AND THE COMMAND FROM GOD,

TO ATTACK

THE COMMAND FROM THE ALL MIGTHY GOD,

TO ATTACK, AND BE DELIVERED,

ATTACK AND BE HEAL,

ATTACK AND BE WHOLE,

ATTACK AND BE HEALTHY,

ATTACK AND BE PROSPEROUS.

I PUT ON THE WHOLE AURMOR OF GOD,

AND PREPARE FOR BATTLE,

"FOR HE HAVE GIVEN ME THE VICTORY."

SAYS THE LORD.

FOR HE HAS NOT GIVEN ME THE SPIRIT OF FEAR.

NOR WILL HE LEAVE ME NOR FORSAKE ME

IN THE TIME OF MY TROUBLES.

I SHALL STAND FIRM IN ALL HIS PROMISES TOWARDS ME

I CAN DO ALL THINGS THROUGH CHRIST WHO

STRENGHTENS ME.

"ATTACK"

THE LORD GOD OF US ALL,

WHO GIVES ME THE VICTORIES,

AND

I GIVE HIM ALL THE GLORY

DEC.7, 2012 RAY A. ROBINSON

YOU CHOOSE TOO, JUST FOR ME

[ELOHIM-SABOTH] GOD OF HOST, THE OMNIPOTENCE

You choose to, Wait for me during my traveling through.

Shed your precious blood

Take on all my sins

Look beyond all my faults

Heal my body when I'm sick

You choose to, Feed me when I'm hungry,

Clothed my nakedness

Keep shelter over my head

Fight for me in battle.

You choose to, Be beaten, spit on, slap

Punched, kicked.

You choose to, Be whipped all night long

Your flesh torn, ripped, from your bones,

Intestines hanging

Eye hanging out the socket

Ears hanging down, your

Ribs protruding and exposed

Your entire body mutilated from

Head to toe.

You choose to, Put on a crown of thrones

Deeply pierced in your

Head, without saying a word

Be tempted by the devil

Lied on, falsely accused of

Blasphemy,

You choose to, Come to this world, to save me

From a burning hell

Be stretched out wide your arms

Nailed to the cross in your

Hands and feet,

You choose to, Be pierced in your side, water and

Blood flowed

Be beaten for my

Transgressions,

Bruised for my

Iniquities

To share the gospel with

Mankind, until I choose,

To choose you as my all in all.

You choose to, Be Crucified Just For Me

Thank you Jesus, for choosing me;

Ray Anthony Robinson Nov.18, 2012

STANDING IN THE NEED OF PRAYER

FOR US ALL

[JEHOVAH-RAAH]—THE LORD IS MY SHEPHERD

FATHER GOD, THANK YOU FOR THIS PRECIOUS MOMENT

TO BEHOLD YOUR AWESOME POWER IN PRAYER.

THIS IS THE DAY YOU HAVE MADE FOR ME

TO REJOICE AND GIVE YOU THANKS UNTO

THE FATHER, THE SON, THE HOLY GHOST.

TO PRAISE YOU FOR ALL YOUR GLORY.

TO LEAD US IN YOUR HOLY WORD OF TRUTH.

THANK YOU FOR YOUR NEW MORNING MERCIES

AND YOUR ALL DAY LONG GRACE.

FATHER GOD, WHO ART IN HEAVEN,

AS YOU SIT ON YOUR EVERLASTING THRONE

I BRING MY PETITION BEFORE YOU;

BLESS OUR CHILDREN AND THEIR CHILDREN

THAT THEY WILL HARKEN TO YOUR HOLY NAME IN

REPENTANCE

CONVICTION

WISDOM.

BLESS OUR HOUSE HOLD [AND MY DOG SNOW]

BLESS OUR FAMILIES AND THEIR FAMILIES

BLESS OUR NEIGHBORS AND THEIR NEIGHBORS FAMILIES

BLESS OUR BISHOP AND HIS FAMILY—FAMILIES

BLESS OUR CHURCH FAMILY—FAMILIES

BLESS US FATHER GOD WITH INCREASE IN YOU AND YOUR WORD

IN OUR MINDS,

OUR HEARTS

OUR SOULS

OUR SPIRITS

OUR HEALTH

OUR FINANCES

INCREASE IN OUR DESIRE TO TRUSTYOU

HAVE FAITH IN YOU

BELIEVE IN YOUR HOLY WORD.

INCREASE IN OUR DESIRE TO ACCEPT

FOLLOW AND LOVE YOUR SON "JESUS"

FATHER GOD REBRUKE THE DEVOUR FOR OUR SAKES FROM

OUR MIND

HEART

DESIRES

WILL

PASSION,

EVEN IN OUR CHOOSING YOU LORD.

REBRUKE THE DEMONIC SPIRITS

OF LIES, DECEPTION, WICKEDNESS

ANCESTORS AND GENERATIONAL CURSES THAT'S TRYING TO

KEEP US FROM YOU FATHER GOD.

IN YOUR SONS FOREVER LOVING, HOLY NAME OF

"JESUS".

RAY ANTHONY ROBINSON   12:26 PM 3/8/2013

HIS LOVE FOR ME

[JEHOVAH-NISSI] THE LORD MY BANNER

Praise the Lord, His Kingdom, His love.

His dying high on the cross and his rising from the tomb

below, with all powers and authority,

He sacrifice his life for my good,

to love me, to lead me, to save me.

What a glorious gift of salvation,

to place me the head and not the tail.

To show me his wonderful and marvelous wonders to perform

in every area of my life.

Embracing me from all my sins, protecting

His most valuable love [me.]

He is teaching me how to walk in his word

in victory, all for his glory.

How to walk with the Lord's words of truth in all purity.

To open my eyes to see His Righteousness;

To open my ears to the sweet sound of "lo I am with you always".

To come in and dwell in my open heart,

making me to be that which was intended;

a righteous and willing servant

in the eyes of the most High God.

For the law of the spirit of life in Christ Jesus hath made

me free from the law of sin and death.

Amen . . .

Ray Anthony Robinson   Jan.3, 2013

HE SAT DOWN

[JEHOVAH-JIREH] THE LORD WILL PROVIDE

HE SAT DOWN WITH THE SAMARITIAN WOMEN

HE SAT DOWN WITH THE MAN WITH HIS WITHERD HAND

HE SAT DOWN WITH THE FAITH OF FOUR FOR THE ONE WITH

PALSY

HE SAT DOWN WITH THE LAZARUS TWICE

HE SAT DOWN ON THE DONKEY

HE SAT DOWN IN THE TEMPLE AND PREACH THE GOSPEL

HE SAT DOWN ON THE MOUNT AND TAUGHT THEM

HE SAT DOWN BY THE SEA SIDE AND SPOKE PARABLES OF THE

SOWER

HE SAT DOWN AND EXSPELLED THE DEVIL OUT OF THE

SYROPHENICIAN WOMEN'S, DAUGHTER

HE SAT DOWN AND BLESS THE CHILDREN

HE SAT DOWN AT THE TABLE

HE SAT DOWN IN THE HOUSE OF SIMON THE LEPER AT MEAT

BEING PREPARED FOR HIS BURIAL

HE SAT DOWN ON THE SEVENTH DAY.

WHEN EVER HE SAT DOWN, THINGS CONTINUE TO HAPPENED

HIS WORK OF SUSTAINING CREATION,

POWER RELEASE

MIRACLES PERFORMED

HEALING WAS GIVEN

MYSTERY IN PARABLES TOLD

PROPHECY REVEALED AND FORFILLED . . .

IN THE BEGINNING HE SAT DOWN AND SPOKE A WORD

AND IT WAS SO,

IT CAME TO PAST,

IT DID NOT RETURN BACK VOID.

THIS TELLS ME THAT HE SAT DOWN ON MY CIRCUMSTANCE

MY LIFE'S ISSUES

MY ENEMIES

MY HURT

MY PAIN

MY SUFFERING

MY AFFLICTIONS

MY BROKENNESS

MY SORROWS

MY DEPRESSION

MY, TRANSGRESSION

MY OMISSION-

MY CO-MISSION OF SIN

MY FILTHY MESSY SELF

HE SAT DOWN ON THEM ALL AND

POWER

AUTHORITY

DOMINION

WAS RELEASED BY THE SPEAKING OF HIS WORD

AND

WHEN IT WAS FINISHED

HE SAT DOWN, AND HE SAID IT WAS GOOD.

LET JESUS SIT ON ALL YOUR TROUBLES,

AND

BE STILL AND SEE

THE SALVATION OF THE LORD . . .

AFTER JESUS WAS ACCENDED UNTO THE HEAVEN

HE SAT DOWN AT THE RIGHT HAND SIDE OF GOD.

AMEN.

RAY ANTHONY ROBINSON   11:15 PM 3/24/2013

CONFIDENT IN GODS WORD
[ELOHIM-ELYON] GOD THE MOST HIGH

BY HIS WORD I KNOW I'LL MAKE IT SOME HOW

It Will Not Return Back Void, He Said It,

He'll Do It, Because He's More Than Just Able.

He's Not A Man That He Should Lie,

Nor Son Of Man That he should repent.

BY HIS GRACE I KNOW I'LL MAKE IT SOMEHOW

Because of His Personal Intimacy With Me And

His loving kindness Towards Me

Through The Redemption of Christ.

BY FAITH I KNOW I'LL MAKE IT SOMEHOW

By His Authority I Can Speak That Which

I Cannot See No Matter How The

Situation May Be, Just Knowing It Is So.

BY FAITH IN THE WORD OF GOD, I KNOW

I'LL MAKE IT SOMEHOW

Knowing his word, who he is in my life,

And the power of his word for my life,

I was already chosen, and anointed.

I Just Believe.

I'LL MAKE IT SOMEHOW

Ray Anthony Robinson   Nov, 07-2012

Fallen

[JEHOVAH-MEKADDESKUM]

THE LORD WHO SANCTIFIES

My life seems empty without no use, void, and nothingness.

My inside is filled with emotional aliens that feed on

My life of emptiness

No control

No direction

No path

No reasoning, nothing to look for.

Being in a box like prism, existing to experience a repetition of the

past only.

Not knowing a present or future of any kind.

Can't remember my history.

Seeing time go by with no expectation of hope not even a little speck.

I hide from the rain

from the cold

from the heat

from the wind

Fearing what it's capable of against me.

My cloudy sky has a white ball, Round in shape but no light shinning.

Where can I go?

What is there to do?

How can I make it through all this zombie, lifeless trap?

No way out. Can't lose what's already lost.

This cycle has no end to let go of.

Weak, fragile, pitiful, degrading, insecure.

Just don't know anymore, somebody or some-thing help me . . .

My dearest friend you forgot your heart

Give it to me and you shall be free.

These shackles

Chains

Hindrances

High mountains

Low Valleys

Storms.

ALL your life's issues and circumstances

You shall see them no more.

But trials-n-tribulations will come

But by faith; you will become a conqueror.

12:37 PM 3/18/2013   Ray Anthony Robinson

I BELONGS TO GOD

[JEHOVAH-HOSENU]-THE LORD OUR MAKER

MY WHOLE BEING, FROM HEAD TO TOE

BELONGS TO GOD.

NOT TO THE WORLD

NOT TO SIN

NOT TO THE FLESH.

NOT TO MY CIRCUMSTANCES

NOT TO MY ISSUES

NOT TO MY MISTAKES

NOT TO MY PROBLEMS.

I BELONGS TO THE FATHER

THE CREATOR

THE ADONAI JEHOVAH

I FIGHT TO GIVE IT ALL TO JESUS, BECAUSE I HAVE

THE TENDENCY TO TAKE IT BACK.

I BELONG TO GOD.

HE IS THE SPIRIT THAT LETS ME SLEEP AT NIGHT,

HE WAKES ME UP IN HIS NEW MERCIES, KNOWING

THAT EVERY THING WILL BE ALL RIGHT IN

MY CIRCUMSTANCES

ISSUES

MISTAKES

PROBLEMS.

THEY ALL BELONG TO JESUS.

I CAST MY CARES UPON HIM AND HE WILL GIVE ME REST.

I SANTIFIED MYSELF UNTO GOD A LIVING SACRIFICE

NOT TO THE WORLD,

SO SATAN CAN'T HAVE HIS WAY IN ME.

GOD IS NOT DEAD,

THAT I CAN DO ANYTHING I WANT.

WHAT DOES IT PROFIT ME TO GAIN THE WHOLE

WORLD AND LOSE MY SOUL.

WHAT MORE WILL JESUS DO TO GET ME OUT OF THE

WORLD AND INTO

HIS MARVELOUS LIGHT OF

THE SPIRIT AND THE KINGDOM OF GOD?

"ALL THAT'S NESSACARY"

I HAVE SEEN THE PEOPLE WHO ENTER INTO THE

HOUSE OF GOD,

THAT HAVE BEEN MANIPULATED BY THE

TRICKS,

LIES,

DECEPTIONS

OF THE DEVIL.

THEIR FLESH IS IMPROPERLY AND UNMODESTLY DRESSED IN APPEARALS.

THE DIFFERENT STYLES,

DIFFERENT LOOKS CAUSES

ME TO BE DISTRACTED FROM THE SERVICE.

EXTRAVAGANT CLOTHING

HAIR STYLE

JEWELRY

BODY PEARCING

TATTOO'S

COLOR

SHAPE

SIZE

BODYCURVES

MOVEMENT

UNCOVERING OF THE FLESH

TIGHTLY FITTED CLOTHING,

DISTRACTS MY WORSHIP.

THE APPEARANCE OF A FINE GOOD LOOKING

MOUTH DROPPING—LOOK REAL GOOD—OF THE OPOSITE SEX

[WHICH IS IN MY NATURE TO LOOK]

SWITCHES MY FOCUS FROM GOD TO THEM.

IT'S AS IF THEY HAVE A CERTIFICATE, A LICENCE, AND A STAMP OF APPROVAL TO DRESS

SEXUALLY,

PERVERTEDLY

IMMORALY

AND

UNGODLY.

I KEEP IN REMEMBERANCE; I BELONG TO GOD NOT TO SIN.

RAY ANTHONY ROBINSON JAN.3, 2013

Shed Your Skin

[THE GREAT ONE]

EL-GIBBOR

The process a reptile goes through is

to let the dead or old skin come off naturally.

In other words, off with the old, and on with the new.

The old cannot be a part of the creature's use.

It becomes dead skin.

It has to come off.

The feel of old and new skin is not comfortable.

So to have the new,

The old nature must come off.

Now certain creatures go through this process repeatedly,

and so do I.

Myself, as a human being I shed dead skin,

Especially when there is a cut or the older my skin becomes.

The old comes off and the new comes on by the nature of

healing, stretching, and shrinking.

It will leave a scar that will stay with the skin

and that scar, has a history.

When I die my spirit and soul separates from the flesh

[the shedding of the old skin]

The Body Deteriorates

Decays

Back to the Dust of the EARTH

A lot of you are still wearing the shed skin,

every type of sin, and there's plenty.

I cannot be in Christ in my dead skin.

When I accept Jesus into my heart

My flesh goes through a vigorous shedding of skin transformation

It's Enduring

Patience

Rebuking

Letting go

Rejection

Denying self

Walking away from all things that are against GOD in the flesh.

I am shedding that dead skin

I am shedding that old skin,

Transforming my dead-n-old skin to new skin in

"JESUS THE CHRIST",

So Jesus can work in the newness of my new skin.

Some will keep the old.

Some will turn back to it.

Some will give up a little and keep the rest.

Some will yield to it all.

But GOD bless the ones who

Shed all their dead skin

of this world preparing for

The new everlasting kingdom.

I am still shedding the old skins.

Ray Anthony Robinson—1:12 AM 8/23/2013

It's God's Peace

That Wipes My Tears Away

That Gives Me Rest

That Holds Me Together

That Gives Me Strength

That Gives Me The Joy In The Fruit Of My Labor

That Gives Me The Victory

That Gives GOD The Glory.

That Makes Me Come Alive In My Spirit

That Only He Can Give Me

That Brightens His Light In Me

That Rest Upon My Heart

That Leads me Into Worship and Praise

That Allows me To Share GODS Word

That Helps me To Know GOD'S Word

That Feeds me Till I'm Fill

That fulfills GOD Promises

That Delivers My Soul

That Is Liken To The Mind Of Christ

That Flows Down Like A Water Fall.

That I Feel All Around Me

That He Wakes me Up In

That Directs me Into His Perfect Peace

That Is Full With His Glory

That Gives me Courage-n-Lifts me up

That God Have Just For me.

That Keeps My Mind And My Heart

That lets me know, The Holy Ghost of God Is peace

HOLD ON TO GOD'S PEACE'

For He Shall Keep Us In Perfect Peace . . . Amen.

"PEACE"

Ray Anthony Robinson   1:27 PM 9/9/2013

YOU DON'T KNOW MY STORY

Hurt-n-Pain With Sinful Stains

Rejected-n-Denied living a Life Wrecked

Used-n-Abused, Blinded to Loose

Talked About-n-Lied On, Every Place I Walked

You Don't Know My Story

Heart Broken, Spirit Unspoken

Non Appreciate, My Soul Contemplate

Friends No Where Too The End

By Myself I Had to Defend.

Drunken Bum, with life's Problems To Come

You Don't Know My Story

Struggles In All My Troubles

They All Burst Like Bubbles

To Blind Too See What's Really Happening Too Me

Don't No How To Be Free.

Caught Up, Tangle Up, Tied Up

In The Sins Of The World

Satan Says I'm His Girl

Living In Hell Then Die And Go To Hell

Now "THAT" Did Not Suit Me Well.

"TO GOD BE ALL THE GLORY"

YOU DON'T KNOW MY STORY

He Tapped Me On The Right Shoulder

I Turned Around To See Him.

But No One Was There

Just A Dark Wall.

I Knew It Was Him, Just Because Of His Touch.

I Felt An Answer.

Ever Since Then For [8yrs] I'm Still Turning My 'LIFE'

Around Looking To See Him.

He Brought Me Out Of Darkness,

In My Moaning-n-Groaning.

He Spoke To The Father Of Us All In My Defense.

"I KNEW HE WOULD DELIVER ME"

He Washed Me In His Blood Spotless,

He Straightened Out My Crooked Walk.

He Gave Me New Words To Talk,

He Directed Me To Himself And Told Me

He Will Never Treat Me Like The World ,

But Love Me Forever,

Because Of The World.

He Did It All Just For Me.

"YOU DON'T KNOW MY STORY"

"THANK YOU JESUS"

"FOR TOUCHING ME"

Ray Anthony Robinson   1:09 PM 9/13/2013   [843—817-8592]

The Forgiveness Of All My Sins

Forgiveness-The Most Powerful Word

When It Is Put Into Action.

A Word That I Had A Hard Time enforcing

When The Time Presented It's Self.

A Word That Carry A Strange, Unorthodox, but

Unique Characteristic of Emotions.

The Emotions Puts Me Between What Happen

And What Happens Next.

Wickedness,

Evil,

Betrayal,

Conspiracy,

Puts A Heavy Burden

Of Sorrow In, My Mind, Heart, Soul.

When this happens, I Act Out In The Weakness Of My Anger

That Dulls The Senses Of My Make Up.

The Way How GOD Expects

Me To Respond To Life's Difficulties Is In Forgiveness.

Forgiveness Is GOD,

And He Looks For ME To Portray His Likeness.

Born Of A Women I Have But A Short Time To Live.

That Is Why I Must Perform His DNA's To My Fellow man.

I Must learn How To Forgive Those That Comes Against Me.

IT'S NOT EASY, IT'S NOT GOING TO BE EASY, BUT IT MUST BE DONE.

God Is Not Moved By The Things Of The World.

And He Looks For me To Be The Same Way In

The Spirit In Order To Best Receive A Better

Understanding Of What Is Being Expressed Out From Troubles.

A Hard Thing To Do, Is Too,

Forgive The Person That Has Put my Environment In

Jeopardy.

If I Could Embrace Everything That Is Of GOD

At Least His Principles,

Then I'll Have The Ability To Overcome Troubles

In Which I Have A Long Way To Go.

But If I Keep Trying And Fail,

Even Out Of MY Comfort Zone

Because It Does Not Feel Good,

At Least I Made An Attempt.

If I Were Able To Count It All Joy In my Afflictions

I Pray To Be Able To Please Our Father.

He Tries the Heart And Have Pleasure In Uprightness.

I Belongs To The Father.

8:06 PM 7/29/2013   Ray Robinson

A father, In The Eyes Of His Children

My Super Hero Is My Dad.

When I Grow Up I Want To Be A Great Father.

From My Point Of View Fathers Are Strong And Brave.

My Father Prays To Jesus,

Jesus Is My Daddy's Eldest Brother And

God Is My Big Father.

I Do Love My Daddy.

My Daddy Plays With Us Even After A Hard Day At Work

Fathers Works Hard To Protect, Lead And Teach Their Child.

Sometimes Fathers Make Choices By Mistake.

Jesus Is My Dads Best Friend And I'm His Buddy.

My Father Stopped A Bad Dog From Biting Me.

He Got Hurt But Jesus Made Him Better.

My Daddy Bought Us New Clothes. Then

We Went To Get Our Haircut.

My Daddy Loves His Family A Big Much.

Our Dad Tells Us Bed Time Stories And Prays With Us.

We Went Fishing, Crabbing, An Shrimping, But Caught Little,,

So We Went To The Sea Food Place.

Fathers Teaches Us How To Drive And Then Buy Us A Car.

Our daddy gives us money to buy plenty of candy and cookies.

Lord, please help my daddy I need my daddy.

Daddy Tell Us About Jesus, Who Is He?

Teach The Children The Way, So They Depart Not From It.

"THANK YOU DADDY"

Dec. 11, 2012   Ray Anthony Robinson]

THANK YOU GOD . . .

FOR KEEPING ME FOR YOUR PURPOSE.

I SHOULD BE DEAD.

FOR SAVING ME IN SPITE OF.

I SHOULD BE IN JAIL FOR LIFE.

FOR HEALING ME FROM THE ATTACKS

I SHOULD BE PARALYZE.

FOR GIVING ME STRENGTH

I SHOULD BE TOO WEAK TO CARE.

FOR PROVIDING FOR ME

I SHOULD BE LIVING IN A SHELTER.

FOR PROTECTING ME THROUGH IT ALL.

I SHOULD BE BOUND IN SIN.

FOR TEACHING ME WHO I AM IN JESUS

I SHOULD HAVE BEEN CALLING ON ANOTHER NAME.

FOR BRINGING ME OUT OF MY DARKNESS AN INTO YOUR

MARVELOUS LIGHT.

I SHOULD HAVE BEEN BLIND.

FOR THE MANY THINGS YOU DID FOR ME

THAT I COULD NOT DO FOR MYSELF.

FOR IF IT HAD NOT BEEN FOR YOU JESUS

I WOULD NOT HAVE MADE IT THIS FAR.

THANK YOU FOR THIS LIFE AND THE NEXT.

"I HAVE THE VICTORY"

AND

"TO GOD BE ALL THE GLORY"

"I'VE MADE IT THROUGH"

"FATHER GOD THANK YOU"

WITH LOVE

RAY ANTHONY ROBINSON

3:25 PM 9/19/2013

INVITATION

YOU ARE MORE THAN WELCOME TO COME AND WORSHIP

WITH US AND EXPERINCE

WHERE HEALING BEGINS AND IS COMPLETE . . .

PLEASE JOIN US AT:

LIFE CENTER CATHEDRAL

7190 CROSS COUNTY ROAD

NOUTH CHARLESTON, SOUTHCAROLINA, 29418

BISHOP BRIAN D. MOORE

THE FIRST LADY JAMETTA C. MOORE

IN LOVING MEMORY

MRS. EVELYN L. ROBINSON

MR DONALD M. ROBINSON

MR. HENRY ROBINSON SR.